CU00704243

Robin's
First Flight
- Wings of Courage

Pengalaman Terbang Pertama Robin

– Sayap Keberanian

May the 'Robin' in each of us find the courage to fly!

Biarkan "Robin", satu dari kita, menemukan keberanian untuk terbang!

i

Learn English,
One Story
at a Time!

Belajar Bahasa Inggris,
Satu Cerita di Satu Waktu!

Table of Contents
Daftar Isi

Hi! My name is Robin.

Hai, namaku Robin.

I live in a nest.

Aku tinggal di sebuah sarang.

3

I want to fly but
I am afraid to
fall or fail.

Aku ingin terbang
tetapi aku takut jatuh
atau gagal.

I see my friends fly.

Aku melihat teman
temanku terbang.

I want to fly too.

Aku ingin terbang juga.

7

But I am scared
to try. I ask for
help.

Tetapi aku takut
untuk mencoba. Aku
meminta pertolongan.

9

Mom tells me to believe I can.

Ibu memberitahu aku untuk percaya bahwa aku bisa.

11

Dad shows me how
to fly. He said,
"It is like this:
think, jump and flap
as fast as you can."

Ayah menunjukkan padaku
bagaimana cara terbang.

Ayah mengatakan, "Terbang
itu seperti ini: pikir, loncat,
dan kepakkan sayap secepat
yang kamu bisa."

13

The tree is tall but
I want to try!
I believe I can fly.

Pohon itu tinggi, tapi
aku ingin mencoba!
Aku yakin, aku bisa
terbang.

15

I think about flying. I jump from the nest.

Aku berpikir tentang terbang. Aku meloncat dari sarang.

17

I fly!
I flap and
flap so fast.

Aku terbang!
Aku kepak
kepakkan sayapku
secepat mungkin.

19

I fly across the sky!

Aku terbang
menembus
angkasa!

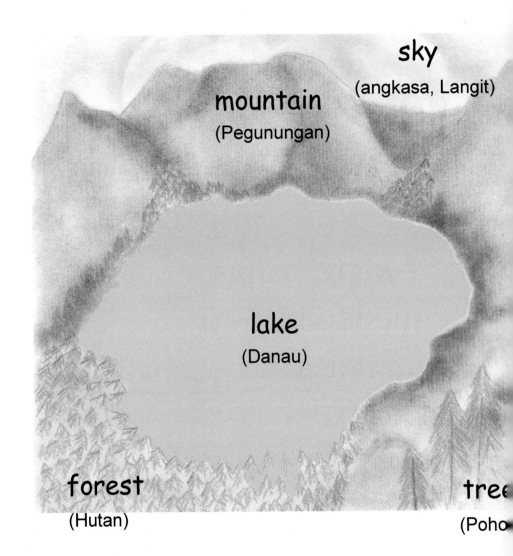

sky
(angkasa, Langit)

mountain
(Pegunungan)

lake
(Danau)

forest
(Hutan)

tree
(Poho

21

Far above the
forest I fly.
The world looks
different from
up here.

Aku terbang jauh
tinggi di atas hutan.
Dunia nampak
berbeda dari atas sini.

I am not
small when
I fly tall!

Aku merasa tidak
kecil ketika aku
terbang tinggi!

Word List

(Daftar Kata)

A (sebuah)
About (tentang)
Above (di atas)
Across (menembus, di seberang)
Afraid (takut)
Am (to be, adalah)
And (dan)
As (seperti, sebagai)
Ask (bertanya, meminta)
Believe (percaya)
But (tetapi)
Can (dapat)
Dad (ayah)
Different (berbeda)
Fail (gagal)
Fall (jatuh)
Far (jauh)

fast (cepat)
first (pertama)
flap (mengepakkan)
flight (penerbangan)
fly (terbang)
flying (sedang terbang)
for (untuk)
forest (hutan)
friends (teman-teman)
from (dari)
he (dia, laki-laki)
help (membantu)
here (di sini)
hi (hai)
how (bagaimana)
I (aku, saya)
in (di dalam)
Is (to be, adalah)
It (ini)

Word List continued
(Daftar Kata Lanjutan)

Jump (meloncat)

Like (suka, menyukai)

Live (tinggal)

Looks (melihat)

Me (aku, saya)

Mom (Ibu)

My (milikku, kepunyaanku)

Name (nama)

Nest (sarang)

Not (tidak)

Robin (burung bernama Robin)

Said (berkata, mengatakan)

Scared (takut)

See (melihat)

Shows (menunjukkan)

Sky (angkasa, langit)

Small (kecil)

So (begitu)

tall (tinggi)

tells (menceritakan, memberitahu)

the (itu)

think (berpikir)

this (ini)

to (ke)

too (terlalu)

tree (pohon)

try (mencoba)

up (naik, ke atas)

want (ingin)

when (ketika)

world (dunia)

you (kamu)

ALFORD
e-Books

available on:
Google Play

Printed Books

available at:
www.createspace.com
www.amazon.com

Please contact us at:
alfordbooks1story@gmail.com
or trythaiketco@gmail.com

www.ALFORDebooks.com

27

Airplane Intro! – From Flaps to Human Flight
Alford eBooks Catalog
All About California – Dreams of Gold
All About England! – Worldwide Words
All Are Equal – From Slavery to Civil Rights
Ant City – New Ideas
Art Intro – With Insects, Eggs & Oils
Bee's Sneeze – Overcome Obstacles
Big Die – Earth's Mass Extinctions
Brief World History – Past Permeates Present
Brit Mu Briefly – From Seeds to Civilization
Busy Bear – Business Basics
Cage Flight – Self Sufficiency
Chase to Space – The Space Race Story
Civil Sense – What if there wasn`t a Civil War?
Computer – Roots of Real-Time
Computers Are Easy to Understand
Cozy Clozy – From Fibers to Fabrics
Easy Science – 7 Eye Opening Ideas
English ABC – Alford Book Club
English ABC – Teacher Guide
English Idioms - Catch Phase Come Froms
Fishi and Birdy - A Fable of Friends
Fun-eral - Last Laugh
G Chicken & 5 K's - Thai Alphabet
Good Food Goes Bad – Why Food Spoils
Hedgehogs Hug! - Many Ways to Show Love
Humi Bird - A Humble Tale
Images in Action - Why Movies Move
I's in US – Essence of America
Jungle Fire - Flee or Fix
Life Then - Applies Now
Meaning of Money - The USA Way
Money Math - With Funky Fairy
Monkey Star - Practice Before Play
Nature's Links of Life
Numbers Count - Not to Nine
Ogs, Zogs & Useful Cogs – A Tale of Teamwork
Queen Jeen - Learns Manners
Read English! - with Red Panda
Robin's First Flight – Wings of Courage
Sand Sea – Full of Desert Life
Science of Everyday Objects!
Senses – From Sights to Smells
Shoe Walks – Understand Others
Smartphone – Objects Before Apps
Space Maps: Trek to Mars
Stars of Days & Months – 7 & 12 Astronomy
Sun's Above the Clouds – A Sunny Point of View
Swim Up, the Waterfall – Be Flexible
Thai Culture On Coins
Too Much Tech – Undo, Over-Entertained
Tree Trips - Wide Wonderful World
Turtle Jumps - A Tale of Determination
Understand Others – Different Words Same Meaning
USA! – Coin Clues
Where Cookies Come-From - Dough to Delicious
Yo Frog – Surprising Songs
Zogs and Cogs – Teamwork (Int'l Version)
Zogs 2 - More Teams

Turtle Jumps!

Money Math

Hedgehogs Hug!

Easy English!
- Signs, Sounds and Sentences

Monkey Star

Shoe Walks

Bee's Sneeze

Too-Much Tech

29

English
ABC
- Alford
Book
Club

Lessons 1 to 7

Douglas J. & Pakaket Alford

30

Teacher
Instruction Guide
Panduan Mengajar untuk Guru

Indonesian
A5

English
ABC
- Alford
Book
Club
Lessons 1 to 7

31

Douglas J. & Pakaket Alford
Translated by Sri Harto

Made in the USA
Middletown, DE
23 July 2017